The Barber Blueprint

What It Takes to Build Success Behind the Chair

By Yusuf ShaBazz

The Barber Blueprint

by Yusuf ShaBazz

Library of Congress Control Number: 2026911433

ISBN: 9781972436974

Printed in the United States of America.

ShaBazz Enterprise Publishing

Victorville, California

Table of Contents

Introduction

Barberingismorethancuttinghair.Itisa craft,abusiness,alifestyle,andformanyofus,a calling.Thisbookwaswrittentogiverealadvice aboutwhatittakestosucceedinthebarber industry,notjustfromatechnicalstandpoint,but from a mindset and business standpoint as well.

Alotofpeopleseethefinishedproduct.They see thesharphaircut,themoneybeingmade,the socialmediaposts,thefullschedule,orthe respectthatcomeswithbeingknownasatop barber.Whatmanypeopledonotseeisthehard work, discipline, sacrifice, consistency, and patience it takesto getthere.

Thisbookisforthenewbarber,thestruggling barber, the barber student, the apprentice, and eventheexperiencedbarberwhomayneed motivationtogettothenextlevel.Itisalsofor anyone thinking about opening a shop and wantingamorehonestunderstandingofwhatthis profession really requires.

Inside these chapters, I share practical advice on building clientele, promoting yourself, making more money, choosing between barber school and apprenticeship, deciding whether to work in a shop or a suite, balancing family and work, and much more. My goal is to give you game that is real, direct, and useful.

Barbering can change your life, but only if you are willing to put in the work. There is money in this game, but it is not easy money. Success in barbering comes to those who stay focused, stay consistent, and stay hungry.

I hope this book gives you knowledge, motivation, and a better understanding of what it really takes to win in the barber industry.

Chapter 1: What It Takes to Become a Barber

Becoming a barber requires hard work, discipline, and sacrifice. Barbering is not for everyone, but if you have discipline and are willing to sacrifice, you can become a very successful barber.

When working inabarbershopasabooth renter, you are responsibleforyourownschedule, and that is where disciplinemustcomeintoplay. When you are not attheshop,youaremissing opportunities to makemoney.Evenwhenyouare tired or not feelingwell,youstillhavetowantto come in and work.Missingdayscanresultin losing clientele andlosingincome.

You also havetolearnhowtobecome comfortable talkingtopeople.WhenIfirst became a barber, Iwasextremelyquietandshy. Once I learned howtoopenupandtalkto customers, I startedmakingalmostdoublethe amount of money in tips alone. However, remembernottomaketheconversationtoomuch aboutyourself.Youwantthecustomertoleadthe conversation.Ihaveworkedwithbarberswhodid not knowwhentobequiet.Theykepttalkingand talking,andIsawclientsbecomeannoyed,stop comingtothem,orstartgoingtoadifferent barberintheshop.Attheendoftheday,you wanttomakesureyourclientisascomfortableas possible.

Last,butmostimportantly,personalhygiene mustbeonpointatalltimes.Ifyousmoke,Ido not recommendsmokingintheshirtyoucuthair in becausethesmellwillstayinyourclothing. Changeyourshirt,washyourhands,anduse mouthwash.Yes,marijuanamaybelegal,and manypeoplemaysmokeit,butyoushouldhold yourselftoaprofessionalstandardatalltimes. Howwouldyoufeelifyouwenttoseeyour dentistandtheysmelledlikemarijuana?Carrying yourselfinaprofessionalmannerwillhelpyou earn more money.

Chapter 2: Promoting Yourself as a Barber

In this chapter, I am going to talk to you about promoting yourself as a barber. When promoting yourself, you should be willing to market to anyone who has hair. If you do not yet have clients paying you $2,000 a week or more, it is not wise to pick and choose whose hair you are willing to cut. You must put in the work.

You cannot compare where you cannot compete. As a barber, it is good to have confidence, but being delusional will not get you very far. One big mistake many barbers make is refusing to cut kids' hair. If you already have a strong clientele and stay consistently busy, then that may be a choice you can afford to make. But if you do not yet have that level of clientele, then you definitely need to put in the work, and that includes cutting kids' hair.

One of the biggest mistakes you can make as a barber is pretending to have a status that you have not earned. It is much more beneficial to actually put in the work and achieve that status than to act like you have already made it. Arrogance will not get you very far in this profession.

When promoting yourself, you should always have a business card that includes your work and your correct contact information. If you live in an apartment complex, you can place a card or flyer on cars. When you are grocery shopping, at the gas station, at the car wash, or just out in public, those are all opportunities to promote yourself and recruit new clients.

Being dressed nicely, looking clean, and presenting yourself well can also help a lot when you are promoting yourself. If your child or sibling plays a sport, that can be a great time to promote yourself at their games and events.

Posting on social media is a good form of advertising, but you should not rely on it alone.

Letsocial media be something extra. There is nothing wrong with using booking apps either, but do not depend on those apps to bring you customers. You need to get out, meet people, and promote yourself consistently. Every place you go can be an opportunity to grow your business as a barber.

Chapter 3: Tricks of the Trade

Greeting customers is very important. It is an easy way to turn a walk-in into a return customer. A good first impression can make a big difference in whether someone decides to come back to you again.

If you are not sure what kind of haircut a customer is asking for, look it up online and go to images so you can get a visual of the style they want. This can help you better understand the client's expectations and avoid confusion.

You want to give the customer as much of your attention as possible. I am not saying do not answer text messages or phone calls, but keep them brief. Even if you have an earpiece in, the customer should still be your priority while they are in your chair.

Dressing nice and staying well-groomed also attracts clientele. Do not come to the shop wearing slides or slippers because it looks very unprofessional. Your appearance says a lot about how seriously you take your craft.

Also, do not pick up bad habits from other barbers, especially if you do not already have an established clientele. Those habits can slow down your growth and make it harder to build your business.

If you are a new barber in the shop, try to be the first one there every day and the last one to leave. That kind of work ethic can take you very far when it comes to building clientele and earning respect.

Chapter 4: Tips on Cutting Hair

Inthischapter,Iamgoingtotalkabouttipson cuttinghair.Oneofthemostimportanttipsisto alwayscombthehairthoroughly.Thishelpsyou checkforanycutscarsorcowlicks.Acowlickis an areawherethehairgrowsinadifferent directionfromtherest.Itisveryimportantto locatethatareabeforeyoustartthehaircutsoyou do notcutittoolow.

Sometimesitisbettertoleavethatareaalittle longer.Evenifitsticksupalittlebit,thatisbetter than cuttingittoolowandmakingitappearasa bald spot.Insomecases,youmayevenhaveto cut thatareainacompletelydifferentdirection than therestofthehair.

Anotherimportanttipwhencuttinghairis communication. Always make sure you understandexactlywhatyourclientisaskingfor. If youareunsure,itisalwaysbettertorefertoa picture.Goonline,lookupthetypeofhaircutthe clientisaskingfor,andclickonimages.Then show the pictures to the client. Doing this can save a lot of time and avoid confusion.

Another tip I would like to share is about lighting. Lighting is very important, but it is also important not to overdo it. Sometimes I see barbers using too much light. When you use too much light and you are trying to create a fade, the lighting can make the haircut appear more blended than it really is. Then, when the client walks outside into natural light or into a setting with less lighting, the flaws in the haircut become easier to see.

You need enough light to clearly see what you are doing, but not so much light that it gives you a false illusion of the haircut being cleaner than it really is.

Chapter 5: Making More Money

If you are a barber and you want to make more money, there are several things you can do. I suggest doing things that are barber-related. I know some people do DoorDash, Instacart, and Uber. I am not saying you cannot make money doing those things, but why become a barber if that is what you really want to spend your time doing?

If you are a barber, I believe there are barber-related ways to make more money. As a barber, you are definitely in control of how much money you can make. It all depends on how much time, effort, dedication, and hustle you are willing to put in.

If you want to make more money as a barber, I suggest starting with the little things. First, extend your hours. If you want tomake more money, do not open the shop at 10:00a.m. There are people upas early as 4:30 in the morning. If everyone has tobe at work by 10:00 and you open at 10:00, you aremissing a lot of potential customers. Open earlier, such as 6:00 a.m. Also, do not close the shop at 5:00 p.m. If most people are getting off work at 5:00, you are again missing a lot of potential customers. Consider staying open later, such as 8:00 or 9:00 p.m. Sometimes working long hours can be difficult, but if you want to make more money, the opportunity is there.

Another way to make more money as a barber is by offering additional services. Enhancements are a service by themselves. You should not be putting enhancements on everyone whose hair you cut if they did not ask for them. First, some people do not like enhancements. Second, some people may be allergic and have a reaction. Last but not least, enhancements are not free. If you are a barber, you should be able to create an excellent haircut without using enhancements. Enhancements should onlyimprove the work you have already created. Byoffering enhancements asan added service, you create another way to make more money.

There are other services you can offer as well. A straight razor service is another example. If you have a decent pair of liners, are a skilled barber, and know how to do a lineup properly, your lineup should already look good without a straight razor. Adding a straight razor can make it look a little cleaner and last a little longer. That is an added service, and it is another way to increase your income.

Always make sure you have proper styling products available. Do not tell your customer, 'I do not have gel. I do not have pomade. I do not have grease. I do not have oil sheen.' Make sure you have the necessary products to style any type of client you may encounter. Adding styling products is an added service and another way to make more money.

After using styling products in someone's hair, explain to them what product you used, why you usedit, and what it will do for their hair and for thestyle they want. Then you can offer to sell them the same products you used. Selling products can definitely make you more money. Sometimes selling products can make you just as much money as cutting hair, or even more.

If you spend more time outside of the shop trying to make money by doing things like DoorDash or Instacart, you are taking yourself away from your barber business. When that happens, you may lose clients because you are unavailable. My belief is that if you are a barber, you should be available for your clients. People depend on you for their image. In a way, you are like a surgeon - surgeons sometimes have to be on call.

Chapter 6: How to Become a Barbershop Owner

Being a barbershop owner is not easy. Make sure it is something you truly have a passion for. If you are doing it just for the money, I suggest you find something else to do. Owning a barbershop can definitely be profitable, but the time, dedication, and sacrifice it requires will be very hard to maintain if you do not truly love it.

Different strategies work for different people. In this chapter, I am going to talk about a strategy I used when I started my second brand. I had my first brand for about 13 years. At one point, I was presented with an offer from someone who wanted to buy my brand. I accepted the offer, but long story short, it did not work out because I never received full payment. I decided to walk away from the situation and let the other party keep the brand.

Idid this partly as a challenge to myself. I wanted to see if I still had what it took to start from scratch, from ground zero, and build a new brand. That is exactly what I did. I started over from the ground up and built a new brand, and today my new brand is ten times more successful than my old one ever was.

The strategy I used to build this new brand is definitely not for everyone. What I did was offer free booth rent for one year - not just to barbers, but also to braiders and anyone else who wanted a booth. Doing this accomplished two things.

First, it taught me not to rely on booth rent for the financial needs of my business. Booth rent should be a plus, not something your business depends on to survive. Make sure you are able to handle your financial responsibilities without collecting booth rent. Once you can do that, you become much harder to stop.

Second, it helped me build strong relationships with my staff. Once the free year was over, I started them at $50 a week in booth rent. Then I increased the amount of advertising I was doing because I wanted to grow the clientele and make sure the barbers were making good money. After that, I increased the booth rent to $100 a week. Then, as the clientele continued to grow through more advertising, I increased the booth rent again to $150 a week.

In the area where my brand is located, I am able to charge those rates. If you are in an area where those prices would not be reasonable, you can still use the same concept, just adjust the prices to fit your market.

When I started this strategy, I had no barbers. Now I have eight barbers. It took me a little under four years to achieve this. Today, I have the top barbershop in my area, the best atmosphere, and hands down some of the most creative and talented barbers around.

Becoming a barbershop owner takes more than just money. If you want to be successful, you first haveto have the vision. You have to have the hustle, the ambition, the dedication, and the willingness to sacrifice. If you do not have those things, and you are not willing to make sacrifices, then I suggest you invest your money into something else. Barbershop ownership may not be for you.

Chapter 7: Walk-Ins Versus Appointment Only

As a new barber, you should definitely be taking walk-ins. If you are a barber making less than $2,000 a week, you should still be taking walk-ins. Once you truly have no open space in your day and you constantly have customers specifically waiting for you all day, that is when you are ready to become an appointment-only barber. That status comes after you have put the work in.

Coming straight into the barbershop from barber school saying you are appointment-only and do not take walk-ins, even though you have no customers, is a mistake. If you are a barber sitting in the shop playing on your phone and turning down walk-ins by telling them to book with you, then you are going to stay that barber sitting around playing on your phone. You need to be taking walk-ins.

Becoming an appointment-only barber takes hard work, consistency, dedication, and discipline. You cannot just wake up and decide that you are at that level without putting in the work, because you are going to end up broke and not making money.

I have been a licensed barber for 22 years, and I stillenjoytakingwalk-insbecauseIlikemeeting new people and gaining new customers. I am also a barbershopowner,soIcanneverhavetoomany customers. I have eight barbers in my shop, so if I ever do become too busy, I have another barber who can take care of the client.

In my barbershop, you do not have to create your own clientele from scratch. I have enough clients coming into the shop that everyone can make money. A barber can build their own clientele and still benefit from the extra flow of walk-ins to make additional money. I would not be abletocreatethatkindofenvironmentifIonly took appointments. I would not have the same motion that I have now.

That is something to think about: do you want the motion? I like high volume and a lot of activity. I also have the skill set to do any haircut in 15 to 30 minutes max. I am not doing hour-and-a-half, two-hour, or two-and-a-half-hour haircuts. Because of that, I do not necessarily need to set appointments. I am also comfortable cutting all textures of hair, so no one who walks in is going to make me feel uncomfortable or unsure of myself.

Chapter 8: Barbershop Versus Suite

In this chapter, I am going to talk about working in a barbershop environment versus working in a private suite. If you are a new barber, or a barber who does not yet have a strong clientele, you should definitely work in a barbershop environment. You should not consider working in a suite until you have built your clientele to at least $2,000 a week or more.

It is possible to build a clientele while working in a suite, but it will be much harder because you will not get the same foot traffic or walk-ins. You will have to depend almost entirely on your advertising. It is not impossible, but it will usually be a much longer process. In a barbershop environment, if you have the skill set, you may be able to build your clientele within a couple of months. In a suite, that same process may take a couple of years. Barber suites are better suited for experienced barbers with a high volume of clientele.

Going intoasuitebeforeyouarereadycan cause a lot of financial issues. Me personally, I enjoy being in the barbershop environment. I like meeting new people, and I like gaining new clients every day. I believe the sky is the limit. I do not want to put a cap on how many clients I can have. If clients are willing to wait for me and book with me, then I would love to be their barber. If I become too busy and they feel like they do not have time to wait for me or do not want to wait for my books to open up, then I have no problem with them choosing a different barber. But personally, I will never turn down the opportunity to be someone's barber if they want to giveme thatopportunity.

I also do not put a cap on how much money I can make. Some barbers work four hours a day. Some work six. There are even some who only want to work two hours a day. I have no problem putting the time in. I work as much as needed.

Everything is not for everybody. I am simply saying that, for me personally, I do not turn down opportunity. I just look at things differently. If I work extremely hard one day, that can set me up for the next few days. I can rest, recover, and then get back to it.

Not everybodyisgoingtohavethattypeof hustle, and thatisokay.Youhavetofindwhat works for you.ButIwillsaythis:barberlifeisfor hustlers. If youonlywanttocutfourheadsaday and charge $500ahead,thatisfine-butyouhave to understandthattogettothatpoint,youwill have toputintheworkandthetimefirst.Ifyou are notwillingtoworkandyouarenotwillingto sacrifice,thenyouneedtoconsideradifferent o ccup ation .

Thatisjustmebeingrealwithyou.Thereis money in the barber game, but it is not easy.

Chapter 9: Barber School Versus Apprenticeship Program

Barberschoolcanusuallybecompletedin seven toeightmonths,whileanapprenticeship program typically takes abouttwo years to complete.Whenitcomestodecidingwhichpath to take, itwillvarydependingontheindividual.

If youhavethetimetogotoschooleight hours aday,donotneedtowork,andhave absolutely no barber skills, then barber school may beagoodfitforyou.Ontheotherhand,if you already havebarberskillsand want to increase your knowledge while becoming licensed,theapprenticeshipprogrammaybea better fit.Withanapprenticeship,youareallowed to workinabarbershopandearnmoneywhile continuing to learn.

If you decide to choose the apprenticeship program,youneedtomakesureyouarevery disciplinedwhenitcomestothebookwork.Make sureyou are completing the worksheets and actually learning about sanitation. Sometimes apprentice barbers pick up bad habits in the shop, such as cutting hair and then sitting down without sweeping up or cleaning their station. That is one thing you are less likely to pick up in barber school. So if you choose the apprenticeship route, make sure you are not developing bad habits and that you stay on top of sanitation.

If you already have the skill set, going to barber school may mean wasting valuable time that you could be using to make money. In that case, I feel the apprenticeship program would be a better fit for you. But if you have absolutely no knowledge of cutting hair, then barber school would likely be the better option. In barber school, you have the opportunity to practice on

clients who understand thatyou are still learning. In a professional barbershop,people are expecting a professional haircut whenthey walk in.

Barber school is also alotmore expensive than the apprenticeship program.Still, if you do not know how to cut hair, barber school is the better place to begin. Going into a barbershop without knowing what you are doing can hurt the shop's reputation and may cause customers to tell others not to come to you. In barber school, you do not have to worry about that in the same way, because everyone understands that it is a barber college and that the students are there to practice and learn.

Aftercompletingthetwo-yearapprenticeship, you willbeabletotakethestateboardtest for your barberlicense.Onceyoupassthattest, you become alicensedbarberandcanworkwherever you choose.Whileyouareintheapprenticeship program,youareconsideredanapprenticebarber. That meansyoumustworkunderalicensed barber, andyoushouldonlybeworkingwhen that licensed barberispresent.

To sumitallup,ifyoualreadyhavebarber skills andneedtomakemoneywhilebecoming licensed,theapprenticeshipprogrammaybe the better fitforyou.Ifyouhavenoknowledge of cutting hair but want to become a barber, barber school would likely be thebetter choice.

Chapter 10: Balancing Family and Work

Balancing family and work can be very difficult when you are a barber. As a barber, there are a lot of people counting on you, but at the same time, you also have family counting on you. You could say, 'Forget about the clients, I just want to be with my family,' but it is not that simple. You still have bills to pay, and you need to make a living. If you are not consistent with your clients, you are not going to build or maintain a strong clientele. That means you have to learn how to balance both.

I think the best way to handle it is by scheduling events and outings during your slower periods. That way, during your busy season, it will be more understandable that you need to work. Of course, some things will come up during your busy periods, like your kids' sports games or other important events. Me personally, I have never missed any of my kids' sports games, because that is something you cannot replace or just do another day.

Now, if my child wanted to go to the movies or go out to eat, there might be times when the shop is busy and I cannot do that right then. That is something we can do on a different day. But the things you cannot get back, you have to make time for. If your child has a game, you take the time off and go to the game.

The same goes for everyday tasks. If you need to do laundry, that is something you can do at three or four in the morning. That is something you can do at almost any time. It is not a good idea to take a full day off work just to do laundry. You have to learn the difference between what can be rescheduled and what cannot.

That is just one example of how to balance your time the right way. You also need to remember to make time for yourself. When you are a barber, it is easy to get caught up in work andfamily and end up with no time left for yourself. I think it is very necessary to make time for yourself, even if that means getting up at 4:00 or 4:30 in the morning to go to the gym. Little things like that will help keep you in the game much longer.

If you do not make time for yourself, eventually you will getburned out and may lose interest in being a barber.

Chapter 11: Bonus Chapter

In this chapter, I am going to cover a few different topics. The first topic is dealing with your coworkers—the dos and don'ts of the barbershop when working with other barbers.

Sometimes, when you work with barbers, you become more than just coworkers. You build a bond, a brotherhood, a sisterhood, more like a family. But even when you do not always get along with the people you work with, you should still show them respect. Greet them when you come into the barbershop. When you leave, say good night and wish them a good rest of their day. Keep it cordial.

Never try to steal one of your coworkers' customers. If a customer comes in asking for a barber who is not there, let them know that barber is not in the shop. You can offer to call them for the customer, or let the customer contact them directly. Always let the customer be the one to ask youto cut their hair. Do not just offer to cut one of your coworker's clients. Give them the same respect you would want them to give you.

When it comes to walk-ins, if the shop does not have a walk-in system in place, be fair. My father used to always say, 'Treat people the way you want to be treated.' With that being said, if you have already cut a walk-in and another walk-in comes in, allow the next barber to take care of that client if they do not have anyone in their chair. Do not just keep grabbing as many walk-ins as you can, knowing there are other barbers there who are also trying to build their clientele. Be fair with the people you work with, and help keep the environment peaceful, calm, relaxing, and enjoyable.

The next topic I want to discuss is dealing with clients. Sometimes, over time,you may build a close friendship with a client.That can happen naturally. However, it is notagood idea to purposely try to make everysingle client your friend. You do not want yourentire clientele to be based on friendship.Remember,thisisabusiness, not a socialclub.Sometimes,whenyoutryto make everyoneyourfriend,theystarttakingyou for granted.Theymaynotwanttopayyourfull price, or theymayexpectyoutofittheminahead of other payingclients.Becauseofthat,itis usually bettertokeeptherelationshipprofessional as much aspossible.

The nexttopicIwanttotouchonisthe barbershop environment. Always keep the shop welcoming and inviting. Do not play music based only on yourpersonaltaste.Playmusicthatis respectable for whoever may come into the shop. You wanttokeepanice,coolvibe.Youdonot want anyonetobeoffendedorturnedoffbythe type of musicbeingplayed.Sometimesyoumay have a certaingroupintheshop,andyoumight play a certainkindofmusic.Butifsomeoneelse comes in whomaynotappreciatethatmusic,it would be wisetoswitchitandplaysomething more neutral.Remember,itisnotaboutyouand what youlike.Itisaboutwhatmakesthe customers comfortable. They are the ones spending their money.

The same goes for conversation. If you are having a conversation and someone walks in who may not appreciate what is being discussed, shut the conversation down and be respectful to the client who just walked in. That customer is spending money too.

Turn on the television, but do not put on only your favorite show. Put on something more neutral for everyone, maybe sports, the news, or something generally entertaining. I usually try to stay away from comedy because sometimes jokes can be said that others may find offensive. You do not want to offend someone who is trying to spend money with you.

The next topic I want to talk about is staying humble. Do not try to become a celebrity and treat your customers like they need you. As a barber, you are someone who serves the community, so do not treat people in the community like they needyou more than you need them. You need themtoo. Stay humble and respectful at all times.

Ifyou choose to be an appointment-only barber, that is your choice. But do not treat walk-ins rudely, and do not disrespect them. Simply let them know that you are appointment-only and that you would be glad to be their barber. Then give them your booking information. It is not just what you say, but how you say it. Make sure you say it politely and not in a rude way.

At the end of the day, even as an appointment-only barber, you still want to grow your clientele and get more bookings. If you are rude to someone who walks in, it is not likely that they are going to book with you or refer anyone else to you.

As a barber, look at yourself almost like a doctor. Most of the time, you need an appointment to see the doctor. But if someone walks in asking for help, the doctor is not going to be rude. They are simply going to explain that an appointmentisneededtobeseen.That is the same way you should handle it.

LikeIsaidinthepreviouschapter, cockiness andarrogancewillnotgetyouveryfar. You may havealittlebuzzforalittlewhile,but I promise youitwillnotlastlong.Youwillfade away very quickly.Ifyouwantlongevityasabarber, you needtohaveagood,positiveattitude along with good service.

Justbecauseyouaregoodatcutting hair does notmeanyouaregoingtohaveastrong clientele if you have a bad attitude.

Conclusion

Barbering is a profession that can provide freedom, financial opportunity, personal growth, and the chance to impact people every single day. But as this book has shown, success in barbering does not happen by accident. It takes discipline, sacrifice, consistency, professionalism, and a willingness to keep learning.

Whether you are just starting out, building your clientele, deciding between school and apprenticeship, trying to earn more money, or thinking about becoming a shop owner, the same truth applies: you have to put in the work. There are no shortcuts to real success in this business.

Barbering is not just about giving a good haircut. It is about how you carry yourself, how you treat people, how dependable you are, and how serious you are about your craft. The barbers who last in this industry are the ones who stay dedicated, stay humble, and keep improving.

If you are willing to hustle, stay disciplined, and make the necessary sacrifices, barbering can open many doors for you. It can become more than a job. It can become a career, a business, a legacy, and a way to provide for yourself and your family.

Take what you have learned in this book and apply it. Stay consistent. Stay professional. Stay hungry. And most of all, believe in your ability to build something great.

Testimonies

"Meeting Yusuf was a turning point in my life, as he saw potential in me and encouraged me to pursue my dream in the barber industry. He gave me the opportunity to learn in a real environment, allowing me to observe, practice, and grow without judgment. He also showed me the importance of working hard for my money and grinding every day for what I want, teaching me that success comes from consistency and effort. Through his guidance, I built discipline, confidence, and a stronger belief in myself, and his support helped me turn my passion into a real path forward—something I will always appreciate."

"I met Yusuf by chance, and he gave me an opportunity I am forever grateful for. I went into the opportunity not really pursuing the money, but more so the knowledge he had of the business. Everything he showed me was a key, a gem I tucked in my bag for later. His strategies for building and branding were based on experience from life. I have learned that experience is the best teacher in life. I witnessed him take nothing and turn it into something, not overnight, but over time."

Author Bio

Yusuf ShaBazz is a licensed barber, entrepreneur, and barbershop owner with more than two decades of experience in the barber industry. Over the years, he has built his career through hard work, consistency, sacrifice, and a deep passion for the craft.

With firsthand experience in cutting hair, building clientele, promoting a brand, increasing revenue, and growing a successful barbershop, he understands both the artistic and business sides of barbering. His journey includes starting from the ground up, rebuilding after setbacks, and creating a brand that became even more successful than before.

Through this book, Yusuf ShaBazz shares practical insight, real-life lessons, and honest advice for aspiring and established barbers who want to grow in skill, professionalism, and success. His goal is to help others understand whatit truly takes to thrive in the barber game and buildda lasting career.

www.ingramcontent.com/pod-product-compliance
Ingram Content Group UK Ltd.
Pitfield, Milton Keynes, MK11 3LW, UK
UKHW062258290726
14090UKWH00017B/754

9 781972 436974